D0936193

BONHOMME RICHARD

The Story of the
BONHOMME RICHARD

By Norman Richards

Illustrations by Tom Dunnington

 CHILDRENS PRESS, CHICAGO

Published simultaneously in Canada.

Library of Congress Catalog Card Number: 76-82961

5 6 7 8 9 10 11 12 13 14 15 16 17 18 19 20 21 22 23 24 25

Ten-year-old John Paul hurried along the path that led to the small stone cottage where he lived with his family in Scotland. It had been a beautiful spring day, and the Scottish hillsides were green with new grass. But now it was dusk and John was late coming home for supper.

His mother stood in the doorway and called to him, "Where in the world have you been, lad? We've eaten already and it's another cold supper you'll be getting. Then it's off to bed."

"I've been down at the shore, watching the ships again," John answered. "I forgot it was getting late."

John loved to spend his afternoons sitting on a hill overlooking the bay. He watched the tall-masted ships come and go, their white sails billowing in the breeze. They were of various sizes and shapes. There were schooners, sloops, and brigantines. There were fishing smacks and great square-riggers. Most of the ships carried passengers and cargo. Once in awhile he spotted a British warship, bristling with as many as seventy-four guns. To John, this was the most thrilling sight of all. He dreamed of commanding a mighty ship someday and sailing to distant ports.

After John was in bed his mother sat by the fire, knitting. His father sat quietly, puffing his pipe. He was tired from a long day's work as a gardener on the big estate where they lived. It was owned by a wealthy man, Mr. Craik, and he did not pay his gardener much money. John's parents were poor. They could not buy good clothes, furniture, or other things for their family.

"John loves the sea," his mother said, looking up from her knitting. "He doesn't want to be a farmer or a hired man like most of the boys around here. He will never be happy until he goes to sea."

"Then let the lad go to sea when he's old enough," his father answered. "There is little opportunity for a poor lad to get ahead in this country. If he stays here he will work for low wages and remain poor all his life. In Scotland, a man who doesn't own land can't earn a good living."

At this time, 1757, Scotland was under the rule of England. The Scottish people wanted to be free to rule themselves. They hated King George and his English government. About ten years earlier they had fought for their freedom under their own Bonnie Prince Charlie, but they had been defeated. The fight had been a hard one for the Scots. The English troops had burned their homes and destroyed their farms. Now times were hard and many families went hungry, but the Scots never gave up their dream of being free someday.

To find a better life, John's older brother, William, had moved to the colony of Virginia in America. Although England ruled the American colonies, too, they were so far away that they enjoyed greater freedom. There a poor man could gain wealth and respect. He was free to be whatever he chose. King George tried to force his laws on the American colonists, but they defied him most of the time. They were determined to run their own lives as freemen.

John hated King George and his government. He wanted liberty, too. He did not want to stay in

Scotland if it were not free. When he was twelve, he asked his father if he could go to sea as an apprentice.

"Aye, lad, if that's what you want. Go, and God be with you," his father replied.

John packed a small sea chest with his clothing and other belongings. He said good-bye to his family and traveled to the nearest big seaport. He went to a shipping office and got a job as a cabin boy on a merchant ship bound for the West Indies and Virginia. A few days later, the big ship raised its anchor, unfurled its sails, and glided out to sea.

John stood on deck in the fresh breeze, looking across the blue water. He had never been happier.

"This is the life for me," he thought. "I will learn to be the best seaman in the world."

In the years that followed, John did learn to be a very good sailor. He studied the duties of every member of the crew. He learned to use a sextant for navigation. He watched the captains under whom he served and studied the way they commanded their vessels.

He learned quickly, and each year he was given more responsibility. Finally he became the captain of his own ship and commanded many voyages between England and the West Indies.

But one year he had a bad crew on his ship. Some of these men did not like his strict rule on board. They decided to mutiny. The English leader of the mutineers attempted to kill John with a bludgeon. John drew his sword and defended himself. The seaman was badly hurt in the fight and died of his wounds.

Although John Paul had fought in self-defense, he would have to stand trial for murder in an English court. John did not believe that a Scotchman could get a fair trial in England. Besides, the dead man's friends vowed they would kill him before the trial began.

John decided it would be better to leave these troubles behind him. He paid for his passage on a ship bound for America and settled in Virginia. Because John Paul did not want the English courts or the dead man's friends to find him, he added "Jones" to his name. In America he was called John Paul Jones.

John made friends with many colonists. He liked the spirit of independence in the colonies. He believed that here a man could make something of himself by his own efforts.

During the next few years the situation between King George and the American colonists grew worse. The King's government passed laws to make the colonists pay more taxes. The colonists refused because they did not have a part in making these laws. They firmly believed that King George did not have the right to make them obey laws that were written without their consent. Besides, the tax money was used mainly to support the government of England and not to help America. The colonists did not want to give money to support a government which did not listen to them.

King George did not agree with the colonists. He did not think they should have a voice in the government. He thought they should obey his laws without question. When he sent soldiers to force them to obey, fighting broke out. The colonists organized an army to fight for their independence. They decided that America must be a free country, no longer under the rule of England. Soon battles were raging in many parts of the country. The American Revolution had begun.

The American troops fought well on land, but the country had a harder task at sea. The British navy was the largest and greatest in the world. Its ships seized or sank many vessels that tried to bring food and supplies to American ports. The Americans had no navy, so they could not protect their ships.

Early in the war, a group of colonial leaders met to see what they could do to build a navy. Since there was neither time nor money to build warships, they decided to buy and rent merchant vessels from private American shipping companies. These ships were armed with guns and became the American navy. Because there were not enough experienced seamen and naval officers to man the ships, a call for volunteers was sent out.

John Paul Jones was just the sort of officer they needed, and he quickly volunteered for service in the small, new Continental navy. All the knowledge he had gained on his many voyages to the Indies was put to use. He taught the inexperienced seamen how to handle their duties on his ships. He trained his crew rigorously, and the men worked well under his leadership.

John commanded several vessels and was sent on many important military missions. Americans were impressed with his courage in battles with the British fleet. His skillful maneuvering enabled him to win battles against ships much larger than his own.

He captured several enemy vessels and brought them into American ports. People admired this daring naval officer, and they began to take pride in the American navy.

France had come into the war to help America, and John was allowed to use French ports as his base of operations against the British. John sailed boldly around the coast of England, attacking any British vessels that he met and bringing the captured ships back to France. Once, he actually landed and threatened the English town of Whitehaven, taking some prisoners with him when he sailed away. This would show King George that the Americans were not afraid of the mighty British navy!

WHITEHAVEN
5 m.

The king of France admired John and decided to give him a bigger and better ship to command. A bigger vessel would carry more guns, and John could fight the British warships better with it.

The king gave John command of the *Duras*, a ship that had once carried cargo to the East Indies. It was an old ship but it was in good condition, and it was fitted with forty-two guns. It weighed nine hundred tons, and it had three masts. John renamed it the *Bonhomme Richard*, in honor of his friend, Benjamin Franklin. Franklin had published a magazine called *Poor Richard's Almanac.* Poor Richard is Bonhomme Richard in French.

John immediately began to look for a good crew to man his new ship. Because he could not find enough Americans in France, he had to hire Portuguese, Frenchmen, Scotchmen, Irishmen, and Englishmen who were willing to fight King George. There were 374 crewmen in all.

John worked hard getting the ship ready for battle and training the crews. He made sure all the seamen knew their duties. John knew that a well-disciplined crew was important, and he was a strict captain. He made the gun crews practice over and over again, to improve their aim. The gunners had to time their shots perfectly because the ship was often rolling up and down. If the ship rolled high, and they did not fire soon enough, their shots would

BONHOMME RICHA

go over the enemy ship. If the ship was low, and they fired too soon, their shots would fall into the water.

Everyone had to obey the captain's commands immediately if the ship was to function well during a battle. Men had to move quickly to change the sails if the captain wanted to speed up the ship, slow it down, or change direction.

In August of 1779, the *Bonhomme Richard* sailed from France on its first combat cruise. John was in command of a squadron, so several other ships accompanied him. They were smaller French vessels, except for one new American frigate, the *Alliance.* The captain of the *Alliance* was a Frenchman named Pierre Landais. At first, John had hoped the frigate would be of great help in battle, but he soon realized that its captain could not be depended on. Landais refused to follow orders. He did not want to cooperate with either the *Bonhomme Richard* or the other ships in the squadron. Sometimes Landais would order the *Alliance* to sail in a direction opposite to that of the squadron and would not be seen for a whole day.

The ships journeyed up the west coast of Ireland and around the north of Scotland. John had so many problems with the *Alliance* that he could not accomplish very much on the voyage. But, along the way, they encountered some enemy vessels and captured them. These ships were sent back to France with a skeleton crew of loyal seamen in charge.

When the squadron was returning to France, they met a fleet of British merchant ships off the east coast of England. The English vessels were protected by two large warships, the *Serapis* and the *Countess of Scarborough.*

"What ship is that?" the captain of the *Serapis* called out over the water to the *Bonhomme Richard.*

In answer, John Paul Jones ordered the American flag run up the mast. To the British captain of the *Serapis,* this was the signal for battle, and he challenged the *Bonhomme Richard.*

The captain of the *Serapis* was confident that the older, smaller American vessel could be easily defeated. He had a better ship. It was newer, faster, and had more guns.

John Paul Jones realized that he was at a disadvantage, but he had no intention of running away. Accepting the *Serapis*' challenge, he brought the *Bonhomme Richard* closer to the enemy vessel.

The gun crews of both ships were at their stations and ready. Immediately there was a tremendous burst of fire from each ship. The two vessels drew closer, raking each other with murderous fire. The smoke from the guns was so thick that it could be seen for miles. On the English shore, thousands of people gathered to watch the battle. Some peered through spyglasses at the distant ships on the horizon.

BONHOMME RICHARD

Jones knew that the British guns had a longer range than his. The *Serapis* could stay at a safe distance and blow the *Bonhomme Richard* to pieces. To fight back, Jones had to get the *Serapis* within the range of his guns. He tried to move his ship closer, but the faster British vessel kept moving away. Two hours went by, and the two ships were still firing at each other. It began to grow dark.

Then the other British warship, the *Countess of Scarborough,* opened fire on the *Bonhomme Richard.* Now it was two against one. Jones signaled the *Alliance* for help. Captain Landais became excited. His gunners fired carelessly, hitting the *Bonhomme Richard* as often as they hit the enemy.

Suddenly, the *Alliance* changed direction and sailed off toward the remaining merchant ships, its guns blazing. The British vessels lay unprotected. The captain of the *Countess of Scarborough* realized that the American frigate would now attack the rest of the fleet. He stopped firing at the *Bonhomme Richard* and set off in pursuit of the *Alliance.* Once again, it was ship against ship.

Jones realized his ship was badly damaged and in danger of sinking. He knew that his only chance to win the battle lay in hand-to-hand combat. He had to board the enemy ship. Again he tried to get close to the *Serapis,* and this time he succeeded. The front of the *Bonhomme Richard* rammed into the rear of the enemy.

"Ready with the grappling hooks!" Jones shouted. His men hurled the big hooks which were attached to thick ropes. The hooks caught the *Serapis*, crunching loudly into her wooden hull. Now the two ships were joined. The men of the *Bonhomme Richard* pulled hard on the ropes. The ships swung around and came together, side by side.

The hull of the *Bonhomme Richard*, badly punctured by cannonballs, was rapidly filling up with water. There were fires burning on the decks. Some of the crew became alarmed, but Jones urged them on.

"Well done, lads," he shouted. "Stand by for boarding."

Jones' men tried to board the *Serapis*, but the British musket fire drove them back to their disabled ship. Dead and wounded men were lying everywhere.

It looked as though the *Bonhomme Richard* would sink before they could board and capture the enemy vessel. Then the captain of the *Serapis* called out loudly, "Do you wish to surrender?"

John Paul Jones stood up straight and shouted over the cannon's roar, "I have not yet begun to fight!"

Jones' courageous words renewed the strength of his crew. They continued to fight. They fired every gun they had. The battle raged for two more hours. Finally a cannonball from the American ship hit the mainmast of the *Serapis*. It crashed to the deck with a tremendous noise, covering the deck with a mass of tangled lines and canvas. Taking advantage of the confusion, the crew of the *Bonhomme Richard* swarmed onto the enemy deck, shooting as they went. The *Serapis* was badly damaged by the fall of the mast. Many seamen were injured. The British captain knew he could not win the battle, and he surrendered at last.

The *Bonhomme Richard* was sinking fast. Jones rapidly transferred his crew to the *Serapis*. They stood on the deck of the British ship and watched the gallant *Bonhomme Richard* slowly sink into the dark sea. The ship was lost, but the fight was won.

Taking command of the British ship, John Paul Jones made temporary repairs, and slowly sailed for the nearby friendly nation of Holland.

When the news of Jones' victory reached America, people cheered in the streets. With the *Bonhomme Richard*, John Paul Jones had proved that courage and determination could overcome all odds. Americans knew that if they wanted their independence badly enough they could win it—even from a mighty nation like England.

BONH ME RICHARD

When the British leaders heard of the *Bonhomme Richard's* victory over the *Serapis* they knew the Americans were willing to fight hard to win their independence.

John Paul Jones lived the rest of his life in Europe. He died in France and was buried there. But Americans did not forget the part played by John Paul Jones and the gallant *Bonhomme Richard* in the founding of their country. Many years later a grateful government brought his body back to America.

John Paul Jones rests today in a place of honor at the United States Naval Academy at Annapolis, Maryland. Thousands of young men are trained to become naval officers here. It is a custom for them to visit the tomb of America's first naval hero and pay their respects. The courage and skill of John Paul Jones has become a glorious tradition for our country and its navy.

About the Author: Norman Richards grew up in a small New England town. A descendant of early colonial settlers, he developed a love of history as a child. He holds a journalism degree from Boston University and has traveled over much of the world in his career as a writer and magazine editor. He is the author of fifteen books for young readers and more than one hundred magazine articles on aviation and travel. Mr. Richards lives with his wife and three children in the wooded countryside of Connecticut, not far from New York City.

About the Illustrator: Tom Dunnington grew up in Iowa and Minnesota. He began his art training in Indiana and continued it at the Art Institute and the American Academy of Art in Chicago. He has five children and lives in Elmhurst, west of Chicago. Mr. Dunnington works full time as a free-lance artist. For the past three years he has taught illustration at the Layton School of Art in Milwaukee, Wisconsin.